DATE	AMOUNT	FROM	TO

DATE	AMOUNT	FROM/TO	TOTAL

DATE	AMOUNT	FROM/TO	TOTAL

DATE	AMOUNT	FROM/TO	TOTAL

DATE	AMOUNT	FROM/TO	TOTAL

DATE	AMOUNT	FROM/TO	TOTAL

DATE	AMOUNT	FROM/TO	TOTAL

DATE	AMOUNT	FROM/TO	TOTAL

DATE	AMOUNT	FROM/TO	TOTAL

DATE	AMOUNT	FROM/TO	TOTAL

DATE	AMOUNT	FROM/TO	TOTAL

DATE	AMOUNT	FROM/TO	TOTAL

DATE	AMOUNT	FROM/TO	TOTAL

DATE	AMOUNT	FROM/TO	TOTAL

DATE	AMOUNT	FROM/TO	TOTAL

DATE	AMOUNT	FROM/TO	TOTAL

DATE	AMOUNT	FROM/TO	TOTAL

DATE	AMOUNT	FROM/TO	TOTAL

DATE	AMOUNT	FROM/TO	TOTAL

DATE	AMOUNT	FROM/TO	TOTAL

DATE	AMOUNT	FROM/TO	TOTAL

DATE	AMOUNT	FROM/TO	TOTAL

DATE	AMOUNT	FROM/TO	TOTAL

DATE	AMOUNT	FROM/TO	TOTAL

DATE	AMOUNT	FROM/TO	TOTAL

DATE	AMOUNT	FROM/TO	TOTAL

DATE	AMOUNT	FROM/TO	TOTAL

DATE	AMOUNT	FROM/TO	TOTAL

DATE	AMOUNT	FROM/TO	TOTAL

DATE	AMOUNT	FROM/TO	TOTAL

DATE	AMOUNT	FROM/TO	TOTAL

DATE	AMOUNT	FROM/TO	TOTAL

DATE	AMOUNT	FROM/TO	TOTAL

DATE	AMOUNT	FROM/TO	TOTAL

DATE	AMOUNT	FROM/TO	TOTAL

DATE	AMOUNT	FROM/TO	TOTAL

DATE	AMOUNT	FROM/TO	TOTAL

DATE	AMOUNT	FROM/TO	TOTAL

DATE	AMOUNT	FROM/TO	TOTAL

DATE	AMOUNT	FROM/TO	TOTAL

DATE	AMOUNT	FROM/TO	TOTAL

DATE	AMOUNT	FROM/TO	TOTAL

DATE	AMOUNT	FROM/TO	TOTAL

DATE	AMOUNT	FROM/TO	TOTAL

DATE	AMOUNT	FROM/TO	TOTAL

DATE	AMOUNT	FROM/TO	TOTAL

DATE	AMOUNT	FROM/TO	TOTAL

DATE	AMOUNT	FROM/TO	TOTAL

DATE	AMOUNT	FROM/TO	TOTAL

DATE	AMOUNT	FROM/TO	TOTAL

DATE	AMOUNT	FROM/TO	TOTAL

DATE	AMOUNT	FROM/TO	TOTAL

DATE	AMOUNT	FROM/TO	TOTAL

DATE	AMOUNT	FROM/TO	TOTAL

DATE	AMOUNT	FROM/TO	TOTAL

DATE	AMOUNT	FROM/TO	TOTAL

DATE	AMOUNT	FROM/TO	TOTAL

DATE	AMOUNT	FROM/TO	TOTAL

DATE	AMOUNT	FROM/TO	TOTAL

DATE	AMOUNT	FROM/TO	TOTAL

DATE	AMOUNT	FROM/TO	TOTAL

DATE	AMOUNT	FROM/TO	TOTAL

DATE	AMOUNT	FROM/TO	TOTAL

DATE	AMOUNT	FROM/TO	TOTAL

DATE	AMOUNT	FROM/TO	TOTAL

DATE	AMOUNT	FROM/TO	TOTAL

DATE	AMOUNT	FROM/TO	TOTAL

DATE	AMOUNT	FROM/TO	TOTAL

DATE	AMOUNT	FROM/TO	TOTAL

DATE	AMOUNT	FROM/TO	TOTAL

DATE	AMOUNT	FROM/TO	TOTAL

DATE	AMOUNT	FROM/TO	TOTAL

DATE	AMOUNT	FROM/TO	TOTAL

DATE	AMOUNT	FROM/TO	TOTAL

DATE	AMOUNT	FROM/TO	TOTAL

DATE	AMOUNT	FROM/TO	TOTAL

DATE	AMOUNT	FROM/TO	TOTAL

DATE	AMOUNT	FROM/TO	TOTAL

DATE	AMOUNT	FROM/TO	TOTAL

DATE	AMOUNT	FROM/TO	TOTAL

DATE	AMOUNT	FROM/TO	TOTAL

DATE	AMOUNT	FROM/TO	TOTAL

DATE	AMOUNT	FROM/TO	TOTAL

DATE	AMOUNT	FROM/TO	TOTAL

DATE	AMOUNT	FROM/TO	TOTAL

DATE	AMOUNT	FROM/TO	TOTAL

DATE	AMOUNT	FROM/TO	TOTAL

DATE	AMOUNT	FROM/TO	TOTAL

DATE	AMOUNT	FROM/TO	TOTAL

DATE	AMOUNT	FROM/TO	TOTAL

DATE	AMOUNT	FROM/TO	TOTAL

DATE	AMOUNT	FROM/TO	TOTAL

DATE	AMOUNT	FROM/TO	TOTAL

DATE	AMOUNT	FROM/TO	TOTAL

DATE	AMOUNT	FROM/TO	TOTAL

DATE	AMOUNT	FROM/TO	TOTAL

DATE	AMOUNT	FROM/TO	TOTAL

DATE	AMOUNT	FROM/TO	TOTAL

DATE	AMOUNT	FROM/TO	TOTAL

DATE	AMOUNT	FROM/TO	TOTAL

DATE	AMOUNT	FROM/TO	TOTAL

DATE	AMOUNT	FROM/TO	TOTAL

DATE	AMOUNT	FROM/TO	TOTAL

DATE	AMOUNT	FROM/TO	TOTAL

DATE	AMOUNT	FROM/TO	TOTAL

DATE	AMOUNT	FROM/TO	TOTAL

DATE	AMOUNT	FROM/TO	TOTAL

DATE	AMOUNT	FROM/TO	TOTAL

Made in the USA
San Bernardino, CA
14 April 2019